W

LEGO® MODELERS

BUILD AMAZING
ANIMALS

ILLUSTRATED BY SEBASTIAN QUIGLEY

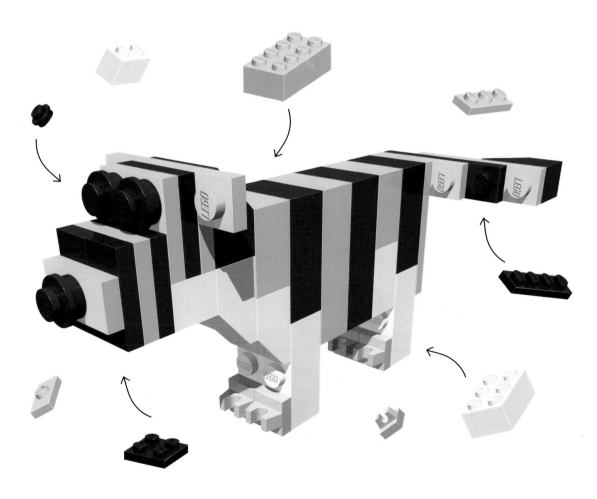

DK Publishing, Inc.

W

LAZY CAMEL

It won't take long to build this camel. But it is very lazy and prefers to sit down!

YOU WILL NEED

1 each of these pieces

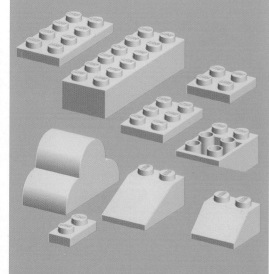

2 each of these pieces

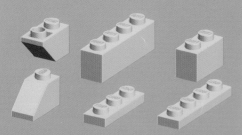

BUILD this model from the base brick upward.

5

4

If you don't have this brick, use your imagination and add another brick instead!

3

Follow the arrow and attach the brick as shown.

2

1

START with the camel's belly!

There are **21** bricks in this camel model.

4

3

2

1

The next step is to make the camel's head.

Finally add the legs.

5

Attach the camel's head onto its body.

6

To make the legs, attach these four bricks as shown.

Finished! After all that hard work, your lazy camel wants to rest. Relaxing is its favorite hobby!

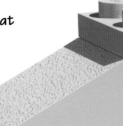

IDEAS

• You could give your camel two humps using two round-shaped bricks.
• You could make lots of different-colored camels.
• Make a camel that stands up by replacing the flat "leg" bricks for upright long bricks.

BOUNCY RABBIT

With its floppy ears and white tail, this bouncy rabbit is lots of fun.

YOU WILL NEED

1 each of these pieces

2 each of these pieces

3 of this piece

4 of this piece

4

Don't forget the big white teeth!

3

BUILD this model from the base brick upward.

2

START your rabbit with these bricks.

1

There are **23** bricks in this rabbit model.

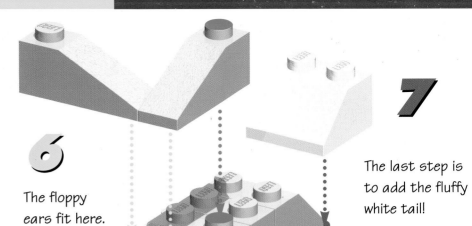

IDEAS
• Change the floppy ears to upright ears.
• Make a warren of rabbits — try making black, brown, white, even spotted rabbits. Rabbits love to have friends to play with.

6

The floppy ears fit here.

7

The last step is to add the fluffy white tail!

5 Add the paws to the front legs, as shown.

This gray rabbit is the perfect pet — it won't try to burrow through your carpet!

CLEVER CAT

This lucky black cat is easy to make. So start right away!

YOU WILL NEED

1 each of these pieces

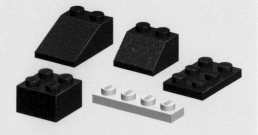

2 each of these pieces

4 of this piece

5 of this piece

There are **24** bricks in this cat model.

Make sure you give your cat a tail!

BUILD this model from the base brick upward.

If you don't have these bricks, use your imagination and add another brick instead.

START with the cat's feet.

8

7

6

5

4

3

2

1

5

4

3

2

1

The next step is to build the cat's head. Remember to add the whiskers!

6 Finally, attach the head to the body. Follow the arrow!

With its arched back and upright tail, this clever cat is ready for action!

BABY ELEPHANT

This baby elephant is still small, but it already has big ears!

YOU WILL NEED

1 each of these pieces

2 each of these pieces

4 each of these pieces

5 of this piece

BUILD this model from the base brick upward.

5 Don't forget these pieces – the ears will clip on here.

4 These four sloping bricks complete its back.

3

Use two of these sloping bricks to make its belly!

2

1 START with the elephant's body.

There are **25** bricks in this elephant model.

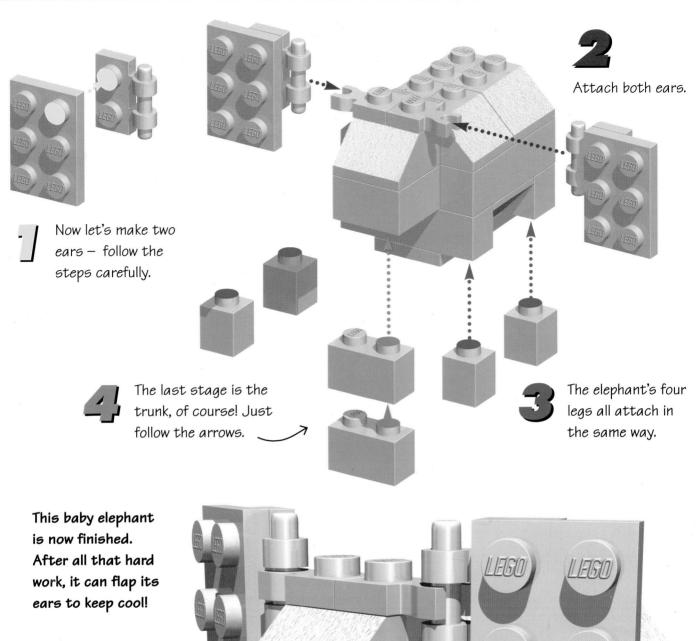

1 Now let's make two ears — follow the steps carefully.

2 Attach both ears.

4 The last stage is the trunk, of course! Just follow the arrows.

3 The elephant's four legs all attach in the same way.

This baby elephant is now finished. After all that hard work, it can flap its ears to keep cool!

IDEAS
- Change the size of your elephant's ears!
- Try making its trunk curl upward.
- Make your elephant grow — give it longer legs!
- Try making an elephant with tusks.

KILLER WHALE

This whale likes nothing better than lurking in the deep waters of the ocean.

YOU WILL NEED

1 each of these pieces

2 each of these pieces

IDEAS
• Build your whale without using white bricks – then you will have a different whale!
• Make a dolphin – build this model with gray or blue bricks.

Finished! But watch out – you have just made your very own killer whale!

There are **25** bricks in this whale model.

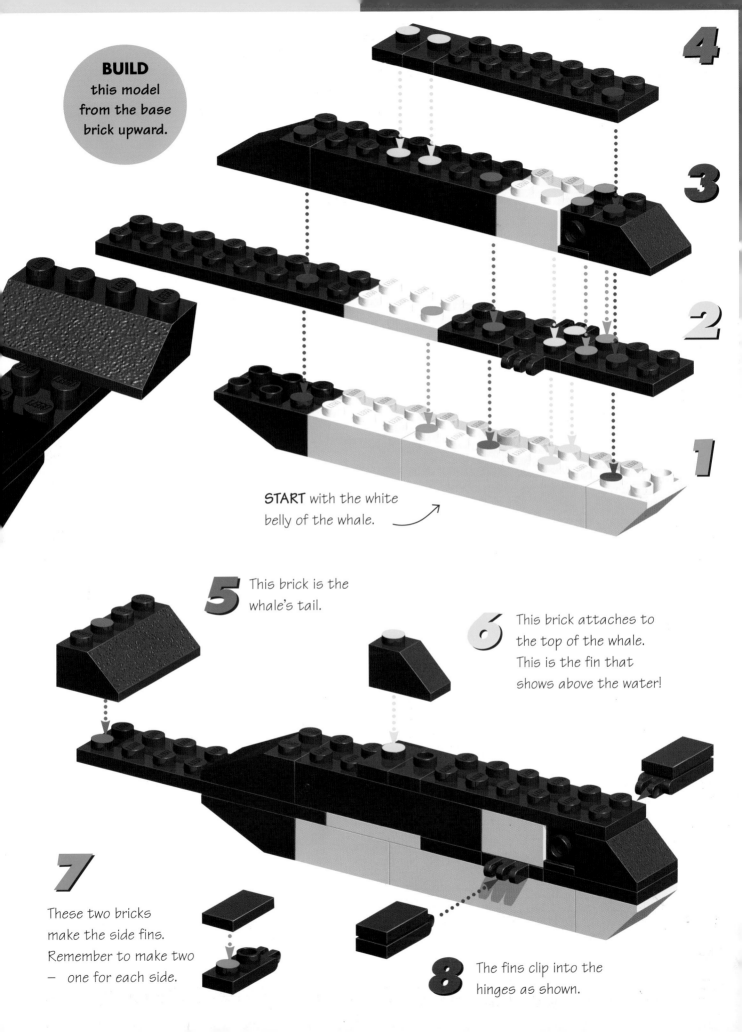

BUILD this model from the base brick upward.

4

3

2

1

START with the white belly of the whale.

5 This brick is the whale's tail.

6 This brick attaches to the top of the whale. This is the fin that shows above the water!

7 These two bricks make the side fins. Remember to make two — one for each side.

8 The fins clip into the hinges as shown.

CRAFTY KANGAROO

In a few easy steps you can build this crafty kangaroo.

YOU WILL NEED

1 each of these pieces

2 each of these pieces

3 of this piece

4 each of these pieces

6 of this piece

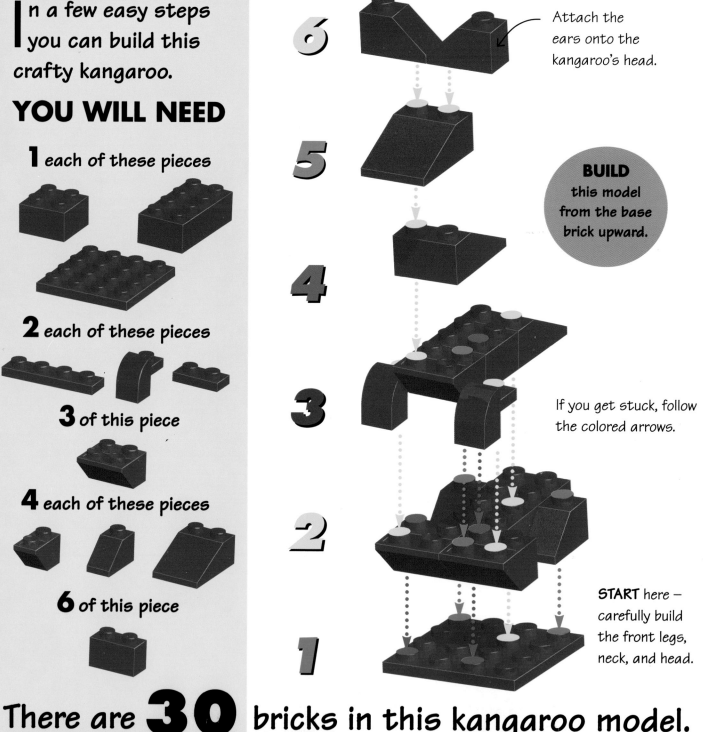

6

Attach the ears onto the kangaroo's head.

5

BUILD this model from the base brick upward.

4

3

If you get stuck, follow the colored arrows.

2

1

START here — carefully build the front legs, neck, and head.

There are **30** bricks in this kangaroo model.

5

4

3

2

1

Last, but not least, give the kangaroo a tail.

5

4

3

2

1

Attach the top of the tail to the body. Follow the black arrow!

All kangaroos need their powerful back legs. But remember — feet first.

IDEAS
• Build several kangaroos in different colors.
• Use longer bricks for the feet to make your kangaroo hop ever higher!
• Add some more bricks to your kangaroo's tail.

This crafty kangaroo is now ready to hop into action!

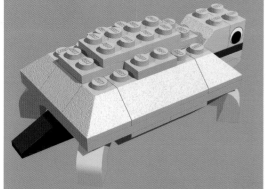

SPEEDY TORTOISE

Far from being a slowpoke, this model tortoise is ready to race!

YOU WILL NEED

1 each of these pieces

2 each of these pieces

4 each of these pieces

It doesn't matter if you don't have these special eye bricks – use solid white or yellow bricks instead.

4

3

2

1

BUILD this model from the base brick upward.

START with this large gray brick.

There are **32** bricks in this tortoise model.

Don't forget the tail!

1

Make four of these legs.

2 Attach the four legs and the lower body to the "shell" above.

This is the lower part of the head.

This speedy tortoise has its eye on you! Be sure to play with it, or it'll hide in its shell.

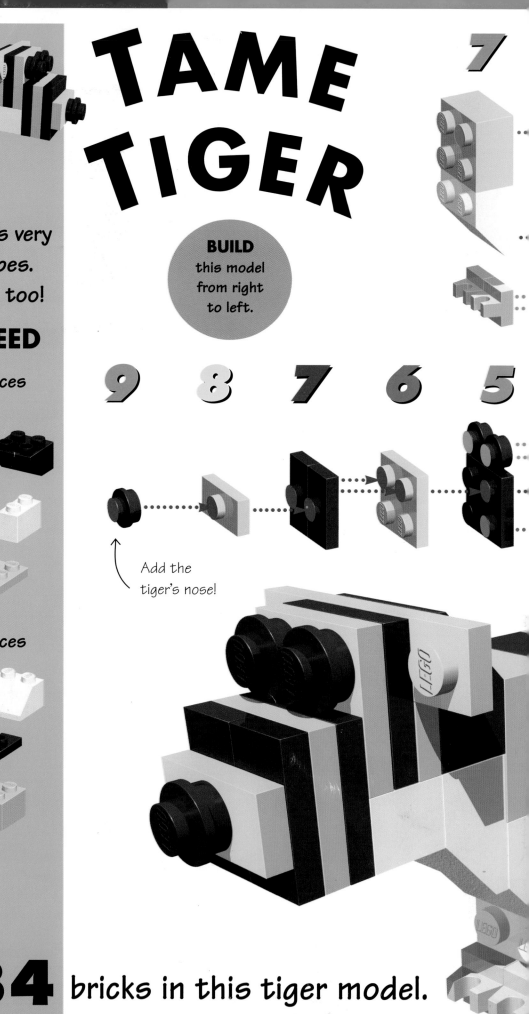

TAME TIGER

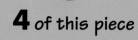

7

This tame tiger is very fond of its stripes. It is easy to make, too!

YOU WILL NEED

1 each of these pieces

2 each of these pieces

3 of this piece

4 of this piece

BUILD this model from right to left.

9   8   7   6   5

Add the tiger's nose!

There are **34** bricks in this tiger model.

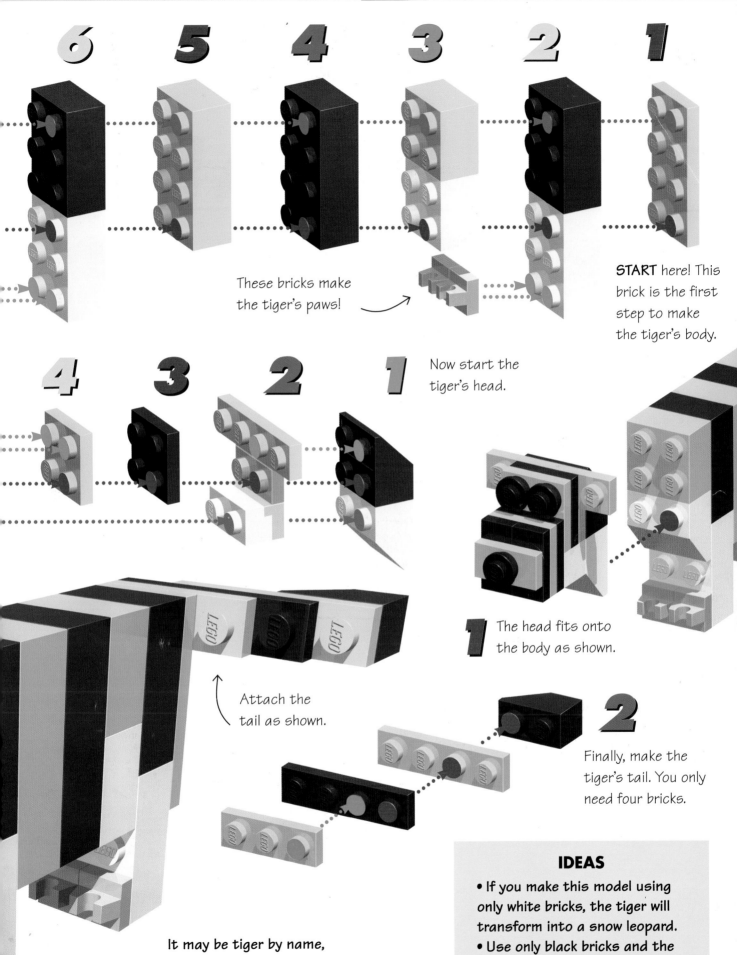

6 *5* *4* *3* *2* *1*

These bricks make the tiger's paws!

START here! This brick is the first step to make the tiger's body.

4 *3* *2* *1*

Now start the tiger's head.

1 The head fits onto the body as shown.

Attach the tail as shown.

2 Finally, make the tiger's tail. You only need four bricks.

It may be tiger by name, but your model is certainly not tigerish by nature!

IDEAS
• If you make this model using only white bricks, the tiger will transform into a snow leopard.
• Use only black bricks and the tiger will become a black panther.

GENTLE GIRAFFE

With a neck this long, a giraffe has a very good view.

YOU WILL NEED

1 each of these pieces

2 each of these pieces

3 each of these pieces

5 of this piece

6 each of these pieces

There are **41** bricks in this giraffe model.

9
8
7
6
5
4
3
2
1

6
5
4
3
2
1

Now it's time to build the giraffe's head. Start with the bottom brick.

START with the body.

7

Attach the head to the neck as shown.

BUILD this model from the base brick upward.

Now your gentle giraffe can enjoy the view.

6

5

Add the legs to the body.

4

3

The legs are easy to make. Just follow the steps carefully.

2

1

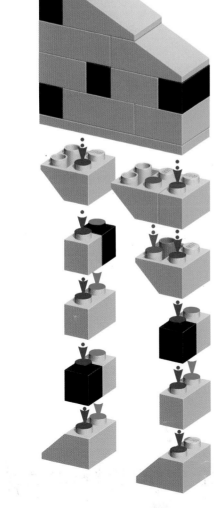

PROUD LION

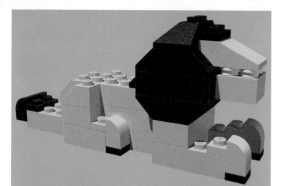

This lion is very proud. When you have finished making him, you will be proud, too!

YOU WILL NEED

1 each of these pieces

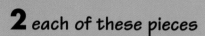

2 each of these pieces

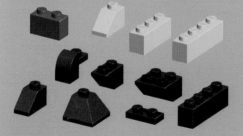

4 each of these pieces

5 of this piece

5

4

The hidden brick looks like this. But remember to turn it around!

3

2

1

START with the lion's body. It is a little tricky, so look at this first step carefully.

There are **46** bricks in this lion model.

4

3

2

1

The next step is to make the lion's head.

5 Attach the head into the gap in the mane. Now you can add the rest of his mane.

6 Remember to give the lion his tail!

7 Finally, make four paws and attach them to the legs.

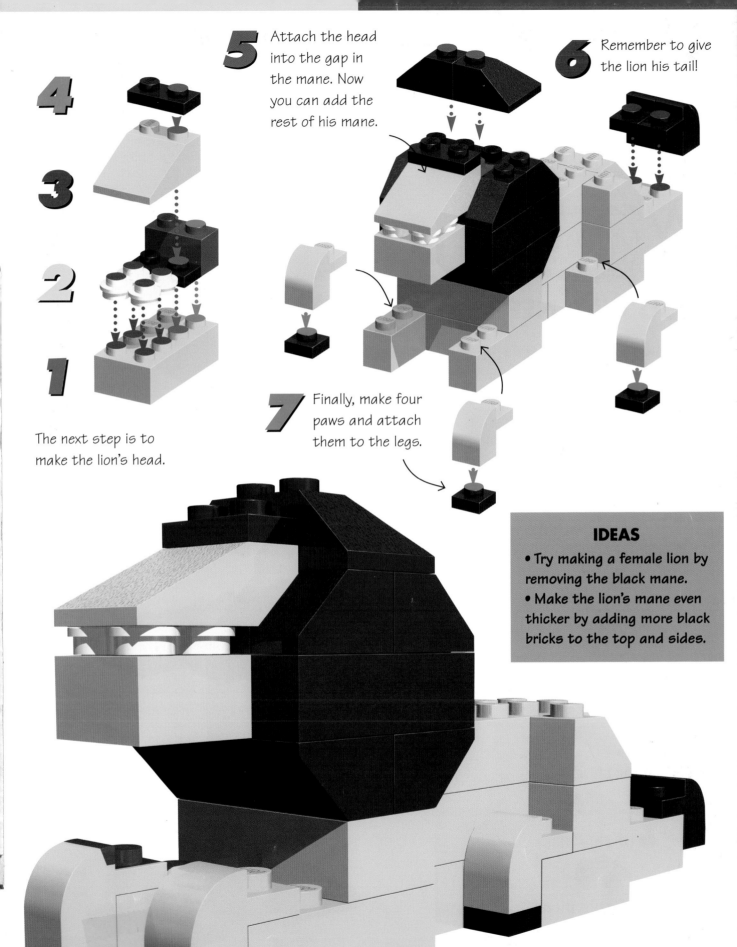

IDEAS
• Try making a female lion by removing the black mane.
• Make the lion's mane even thicker by adding more black bricks to the top and sides.

This lion is very pleased with himself. He is king of the jungle!

FAT FROG

Watch out for this fat frog – he is always hopping around.

YOU WILL NEED

1 each of these pieces

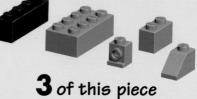

2 each of these pieces

3 of this piece

4 each of these pieces

5 of this piece

6 of this piece

9 of this piece

There are **49** bricks in this frog model.

7

6

5

4

3

2

1

BUILD this model from the base brick upward.

Don't worry if you can't find exactly the same bricks – use your imagination!

START with the frog's body and back legs.

3

2

1

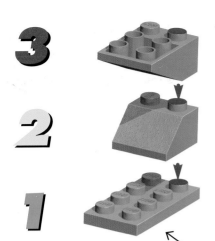

Now make two of these squat front legs.

4

Give your frog two eyes.

Add the last pieces to complete the back legs.

5

IDEAS

• Turn your frog into a toad by adding extra single gray bricks onto the back of the body. This will make the model look more toady!

6

Finally, attach the two front legs to the frog's body.

This big green frog loves jumping around in search of food!

GIANT GORILLA

This giant gorilla is a strong animal. It is a tough model, too!

YOU WILL NEED

1 each of these pieces

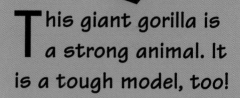

2 each of these pieces

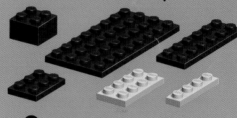

3 of this piece

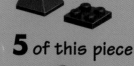

4 each of these pieces

5 of this piece

8 each of these pieces

There are **50** bricks in this gorilla model.

7

6

Look carefully at this stage – remember to add the gray brick.

5

4

3

2

1

START with the gorilla's body. These bricks are the belly!

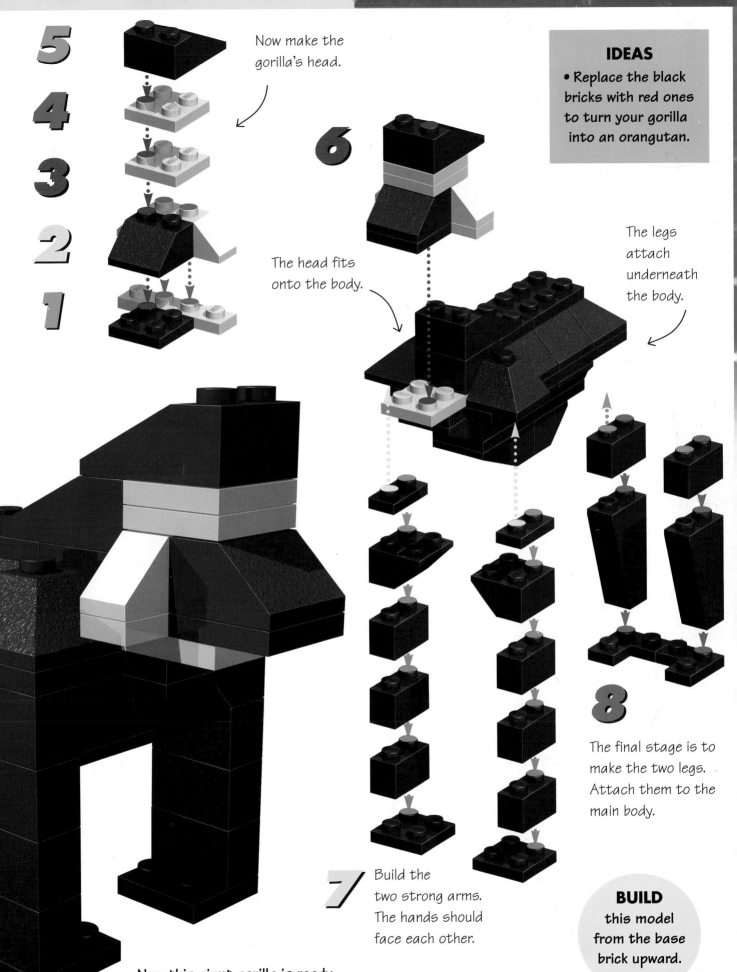

5
4
3
2
1

Now make the gorilla's head.

IDEAS
• Replace the black bricks with red ones to turn your gorilla into an orangutan.

6

The head fits onto the body.

The legs attach underneath the body.

8

The final stage is to make the two legs. Attach them to the main body.

7 Build the two strong arms. The hands should face each other.

BUILD this model from the base brick upward.

Now this giant gorilla is ready to take on any challenge!

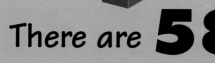

DOPEY DOG

This dog may look dopey, but watch out for his moving jaws!

YOU WILL NEED

1 each of these pieces

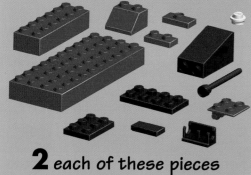

2 each of these pieces

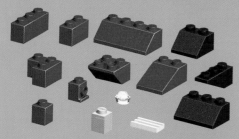

3 of this piece

4 each of these pieces

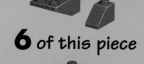

6 of this piece

There are **58** bricks in this dog model.

9
8
7
6

Two of these bricks are hidden. The tail will attach here later.

5
4
3
2
1

START by making the dog's legs and lower body.

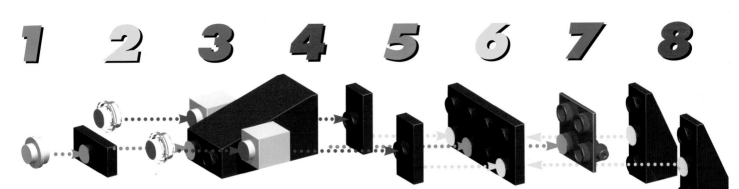

1 **2** **3** **4** **5** **6** **7** **8**

Now make the dog's head – nose first!

BUILD the head from left to right.

Now attach the head to the body. This red brick at the back of the dog's head fits onto the black brick at the top of the body.

9

Finally, make the tail and attach it to the back of the body.

10

This dog's mouth can open and shut!

IDEAS
• Give your dog longer legs and use gray bricks. Then you can transform this dachshund into a greyhound.

This dog loves being the center of attention. So make sure you remember to play with it!

ATHLETIC ANTELOPE

Antelopes **A**run very fast, especially when they're being chased!

YOU WILL NEED

1 each of these pieces

2 each of these pieces

3 of this piece

4 each of these pieces

6 of this piece

These gray swords make the ideal pair of horns!

BUILD this model from the base brick upward.

8

Make the hinge by attaching these two bricks.

7

6

5

Make the antelope's nose with these three black bricks.

4

3

Remember to attach this brick!

Now make the body.

2

1

START this model with the antelope's neck.

There are **60** bricks in this antelope model.

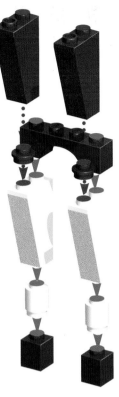

5
4
3
2
1

These front legs fit together as shown above.

These are the back legs.

 Attach the head to the body.

This special antelope needs to be cared for — make sure you keep it safe from prowling lions!

7 The last step is to attach the legs — just follow the arrows.

POLAR BEAR

Polar bears are very big and take a long time to make!

YOU WILL NEED

1 each of these pieces

2 each of these pieces

3 each of these pieces

4 each of these pieces

5 of this piece

There are **67** bricks in this polar bear model.

6

5

4

3

2

1

Look carefully – there are two layers of bricks here.

START with these three bricks.

3

There are two layers of bricks here.

2

1

Now finish making the bear's body.

Your polar bear is almost complete!

BUILD
this model from the base brick upward.

4 Finally, make the legs and attach them to the body.

This polar bear will be camouflaged against the snow. Only its black nose gives it away!

IDEAS
• Use only brown bricks to make a grizzly bear.

To find out how you can purchase LEGO toys on-line visit:

www.legoworldshop.com

THE LEGO BOOK RANGE ALSO INCLUDES:

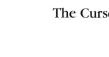

LEGO MODELERS:
Build Fabulous Figures

ROAD MAZE GAME BOOKS:
Spy Catcher
Jewel Thief

PUZZLE STORYBOOKS:
The Lost Temple
Rock Raiders
Castle Mystery
The Curse of the Mummy

Treasure Smuggler
Gold Robber

ALSO LOOK FOR:
The Ultimate LEGO Book

DK

A DK PUBLISHING BOOK
www.dk.com

Text copyright © 1999 LEGO Group
Illustrations © 1999 LEGO Group
Art Editor: Goldberry Broad
Project Editor: Rebecca Smith
Managing Art Editor: Cathy Tincknell
Managing Editor: Joanna Devereux
DTP Designer: Jill Bunyan
Production: Steve Lang

First American Edition, 1999
2 4 6 8 10 9 7 5 3 1

Published in the United States by
DK Publishing, Inc.
95 Madison Avenue
New York, New York 10016

A CIP catalog record for this book is available from the Library of Congress.

ISBN 0-78994-4775-4

Color reproduction by Media Development
Printed and bound in Italy by L.E.G.O.

4/11 12/04 3-1-05